DATE DUE

Demco No. 62-0549

SONGHAY

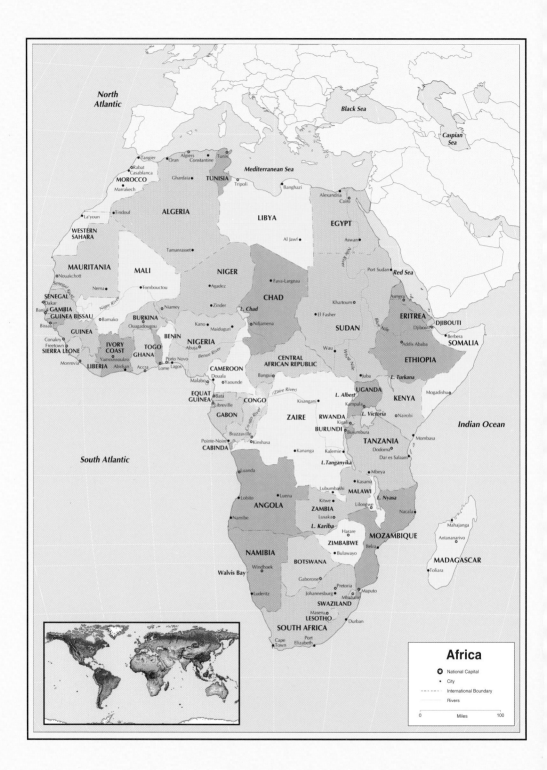

North
Atlantic

Black Sea

Caspian
Sea

Mediterranean Sea

Tangier
Rabat
Casablanca
MOROCCO
Marrakech

Algiers
Oran
Constantine
Tunis

TUNISIA
Ghardaia

Tripoli

Banghazi

Alexandria
Cairo

La'youn

Tindouf

ALGERIA

LIBYA

EGYPT

WESTERN
SAHARA

Tamanrasset

Al Jawf

Aswan

MAURITANIA

MALI

NIGER

Nile River

Port Sudan   Red Sea

Nouakchott

Nema

Tombouctou

Agadez

Faya-Largeau

Khartoum

Asmera

ERITREA

DJIBOUTI

Senegal River
SENEGAL
Banjul GAMBIA
GUINEA BISSAU
Bissau

Niger River

Zinder

CHAD

L. Chad

Blue Nile

El Fasher

Djibouti

Berbera

Dakar

Niamey

Ndjamena

SUDAN

Addis Ababa

SOMALIA

Bamako

BURKINA

Kano

Conakry
Freetown
SIERRA LEONE
Monrovia
LIBERIA

GUINEA

Ouagadougou

BENIN

Maiduguri

Mogadishu

IVORY
COAST

TOGO
GHANA

NIGERIA
Abuja

CENTRAL
AFRICAN REPUBLIC

White Nile

ETHIOPIA

L. Turkana

Yamoussoukro
Abidjan
Accra
Lome
Porto Novo
Lagos

Benue River

Wau

Juba

Malabo
EQUAT
GUINEA
Bata
Libreville

CAMEROON
Douala
Yaounde

Bangui

(Zaire River)

Kisangani

L. Albert

UGANDA

Kampala

KENYA

Nairobi

Mombasa

Indian Ocean

GABON

Congo River

CONGO

ZAIRE

RWANDA
Kigali
BURUNDI
Bujumbura

L. Victoria

South Atlantic

Brazzaville
Pointe-Noire
Kinshasa
CABINDA

Kananga

Kalemie

TANZANIA
Dodoma

Dar es Salaam

L.Tanganyika

Mbeya

Luanda

Kasama

Lubumbashi

MALAWI

Lobito
Luena

Kitwe

L. Nyasa

Nacala

Namibe

ANGOLA

ZAMBIA
Lusaka

Lilongwe

Mahajanga

L. Kariba

Antananarivo

NAMIBIA

Harare
ZIMBABWE
Bulawayo

MOZAMBIQUE
Beira

MADAGASCAR

Walvis Bay

Windhoek

BOTSWANA

Toliara

Luderitz

Gaborone

Pretoria
Johannesburg
Maputo
SWAZILAND
Mbabane
Maseru
LESOTHO
Durban

SOUTH AFRICA

Cape
Town

Port
Elizabeth

Africa

⊗ National Capital
• City
---- International Boundary
—— Rivers

0   Miles   100

SONGHAY

Tunde Adeleke, Ph.D.

THE ROSEN PUBLISHING GROUP, INC.
NEW YORK

Published in 1996 by The Rosen Publishing Group, Inc.
29 East 21st Street, New York, NY 10010

Copyright 1996 by The Rosen Publishing Group, Inc.

First Edition

Manufactured in the United States of America

Library of Congress Cataloging-in-Publication Data

Adeleke, Tunde.
     Songhay / Tunde Adeleke. — 1st ed.
        p.   cm. — (The Heritage library of African peoples)
     Includes bibliographical references and index.
     ISBN 0-8239-1986-2
     1. Songhay (African people)—History—Juvenile literature.
2. Songhay (African people)—Social life and customs—Juvenile
literature.   I. Title.   II. Series.
DT530.5.S65A34   1996
960′.04965—dc20   95-1272
                                                          CIP

Contents

INTRODUCTION

THERE IS EVERY REASON FOR US TO KNOW something about Africa and to understand its past and the way of life of its peoples. Africa is a rich continent that has for centuries provided the world with art, culture, labor, wealth, and natural resources. It has vast mineral deposits, fossil fuels, and commercial crops.

But perhaps most important is the fact that fossil evidence indicates that human beings originated in Africa. The earliest traces of human beings and their tools are almost two million years old. Their descendants have migrated throughout the world. To be human is to be of African descent.

The experiences of the peoples who stayed in Africa are as rich and as diverse as of those who established themselves elsewhere. This series of books describes their environment, their modes of subsistence, their relationships, and their customs and beliefs. The books present the variety of languages, histories, cultures, and religions that are to be found on the African continent. They demonstrate the historical linkages between African peoples and the way contemporary Africa has been affected by European colonial rule.

Africa is large, complex, and diverse. It encompasses an area of more than 11,700,000

square miles. The United States, Europe, and India could fit easily into it. The sheer size is an indication of the continent's great variety in geography, terrain, climate, flora, fauna, peoples, languages, and cultures.

Much of contemporary Africa has been shaped by European colonial rule, industrialization, urbanization, and the demands of a world economic system. For more than seventy years, large regions of Africa were ruled by Great Britain, France, Belgium, Portugal, and Spain. African peoples from various ethnic, linguistic, and cultural backgrounds were brought together to form colonial states.

For decades Africans struggled to gain their independence. It was not until after World War II that the colonial territories became independent African states. Today, almost all of Africa is ruled by Africans. Large numbers of Africans live in modern cities. Rural Africa is also being transformed, and yet its people still engage in many of their customs and beliefs.

Contemporary circumstances and natural events have not always been kind to ordinary Africans. Today, however, new popular social movements and technological innovations pose great promise for future development.

George C. Bond, Ph.D., Director
Institute of African Studies
Columbia University, New York

Many Songhay continue to live in the cities that were important centers of the Songhay Empire. These Songhay girls from Jenne are going around their neighborhood selling homemade treats of peanut butter, honey, and millet.

HISTORY OF THE SONGHAY

THE SONGHAY (SOMETIMES SPELLED
Songhai) are one of the most prominent ethnic
groups in African history. They founded one of
the great empires of medieval Africa. They also
dominated much of present-day West Africa
from the 1200s through the 1500s.

At the height of its power in the early 1500s,
the Songhay Empire stretched from the Atlantic
Ocean in the west to Hausaland in northern
Nigeria in the east, a region called the Western
Sudan. Its territory was much larger than, and
included much of, the territories of two great
empires, the Soninke Empire of Ghana and the
Malinke Empire of Mali.

Today, the Songhay number about one
million and are found in the Republics of Mali,
Niger, Benin, and Burkina Faso. The greatest
number of Songhay can be found in Mali and

This map shows the Songhay Empire colored in light green. Important trade routes are marked by the green lines. Trade in this region was also the basis for the two empires that existed in this region before Songhay: Mali and Ghana. These earlier empires are colored in darker greens. Important gold-producing regions were Bambuk and Bure. The coastal forest regions, the Savanna grasslands, the dry Sahel, and the Sahara Desert each produced different items that were transported along the trade routes.

Niger. Songhay is the second most important language in Niger, after Hausa. In Mali, the Songhay are the fourth largest ethnic group after Bamana, Fulani, and Marka. In eastern Mali, about 400,000 Songhay are concentrated along the Niger River bend. In Niger, they are found mostly in the southwestern villages of Mehanna, Tillaberi, and Wanzerbe. In Mali and Niger, the Songhay are primarily fishermen and farmers, who grow crops such as millet, rice, and sorghum.

The Songhay are a hospitable people who are proud of their history and heritage. They have a deep respect for their ancestors and the achievements of their civilization. They have never lost touch with ancient Songhay traditions. They practice traditional religion and divination. Their cultural values are influenced by both spiritual and nonreligious forces.

The original home of the Songhay people is Dendi, on the great bend of the Niger River. Dendi lies upstream from the present Nigeria-Benin frontier. Historians are not certain exactly when the Songhay migrated to Dendi, but we know that they have lived on this part of the Niger River for much more than a thousand years. Farmers, fishermen, hunters, traders, craftsmen, and warriors migrated into the area in ancient times. It is from the mixture of these various peoples that the Songhay emerged.

Farming in rural areas has always been an important part of the Songhay economy, together with trade in the cities. Here Hamadi Mama Cissé, a Songhay farmer from a small village a few miles north of Jenne, tends his rice crop.

Historians have identified at least three ethnic groups that joined to make up the early Songhay. They were the Gow or Gobibi, who earned a reputation as "masters of the soil"; the Do, who were farmers, cattle-herders, and hunters; and the Sorko, called "masters of the river" because of their expertise in fishing and canoeing. The Gow and Do appear to have been the first groups to occupy Dendi. The Sorko came later. The three groups lived in Dendi for hundreds of years, but argued and often waged war against each other. After years of conflict, the warlike Sorko came to dominate the others.

Little is known of the culture of the Songhay during this early period.

▼ THE ZA DYNASTY ▼

Sorko dominance ended in the seventh century when Dendi was defeated by the nomadic Tuareg people from Libya. They were led by Za Aliamen. The Tuareg made their capital at Kukya, north of Dendi and on the northwestern frontier of present-day Nigeria. Za Aliamen became king, establishing Songhay's first dynasty. The Sorko emigrated farther north to Gao to set up an independent state. In 1010 AD Gao was invaded and captured by the Tuareg, who moved their capital there. The Tuareg intermarried with the Songhay and were soon absorbed into the Songhay culture.

Gao became the center of the Songhay Empire.

Gao had existed as a town since the seventh century, possibly even earlier. Its position was important because of its location in the heart of the fertile savanna. Gao was in the heart of the great trans-Saharan trade network that linked North Africa and Arabia, the Western Sudan, and the forest region to the south.

From about the third or fourth century, Arab traders from North Africa and the Middle East began crossing the Sahara Desert. They brought such goods as ornaments, jewels, sugar, glass-ware, salt, weapons, and horses to exchange for the gold, slaves, kolanuts, and ivory of the savanna and forest regions. This trade lasted until the early twentieth century and brought great wealth to the individuals and states involved.

The people of Gao enjoyed a high standard of living. Their position along the bend of the Niger was an advantage. The Niger River provided good fishing and water for irrigation farming. Because the Niger flows through many different regions, trade items from these regions can be exchanged by boat. Gao soon developed into a small but wealthy kingdom.

The Arabs brought not only Middle Eastern and Mediterranean goods, but also the religion of Islam. Islam was founded by the prophet Muhammad in Mecca in the sixth century. It teaches monotheism, the belief in only one

The Niger River provides water and allows trade items to be transported in boats. Here a large river boat leaves for Jenne while onlookers watch beside their canoe.

God, called Allah. Muhammad and his followers spread Islam through a combination of preaching and *jihad* (holy war). By the beginning of the eleventh century, a large number of Muslim Arabs had settled in Gao. They first concentrated on trading and commercial activities. Soon they began to preach among the Songhay. In 1009, Za Kossoi became the first Songhay ruler to convert to Islam. Za Kossoi encouraged his people to accept the new faith. He also adopted other customs from North Africa, such as the *shaduff* (a hoist for irrigation used on the River Nile), the use of animal manure as fertilizer, and the milking of cattle.

Though their king accepted Islam, the Songhay people refused to part with their traditional beliefs. Islam and traditional Songhay religion coexisted. By the beginning of the

1300s, Gao's wealth and strategic location attracted the interest of the more powerful neighboring empire of Mali. In 1325, Gao was invaded by the forces of Mansa Musa, emperor of Mali, and absorbed into the Mali Empire.

As was the custom in the Western Sudan, two Songhay princes, Ali Kolon and Suleiman Nar, left Gao to live at the court of Mansa Musa. This custom forced the princes' parents to be loyal to Mansa Musa. It also provided the princes with administrative and military training. Ali Kolon remained loyal to the Songhay and hated being in Mali.

▼ THE SUNNI DYNASTY ▼

After the death of Mansa Musa in 1346, a series of weak and ineffective rulers gave the Songhay princes an opportunity. They fled back to Gao, where Ali Kolon started a successful revolt against Mali. Ali Kolon took the title of Sunni, meaning liberator. This was the beginning of the second Songhay dynasty.

The Empire of Mali appears to have regained its power over Songhay for a brief period. But Songhay gained final independence toward the end of the 1300s. By 1400 the Songhay cavalry raided Niani, the Mali capital.

Little is known of the reign of Ali Kolon or of the sixteen members of his dynasty who followed him. For several decades the Songhay appear to have concentrated on building up their

economy through trade, agriculture, fishing, hunting, and nomadic herding. Their prosperity was made possible by the unity they created among many different peoples in the region. Together they fought off repeated attacks from the Tuareg and the Mossi people.

▼ SUNNI ALI, 1464–1492 ▼

Sunni Ali is considered the real founder of the Songhay Empire. Sunni Ali was a man of courage, intelligence, and strict discipline. He realized the importance of the military for the political stability and survival of the state. He also took full advantage of the Niger River by building a navy under a naval commander, the Hikoy. His military campaigns transformed Songhay from a small kingdom into the largest empire in medieval Africa.

Sunni Ali, also called Ber (meaning "the great"), hailed from a strong traditional background. According to legend, he learned to use spiritual powers from his mother and was introduced to the powerful spiritualists of Kukya by his father. When he came to power, he was considered one of the most powerful spiritualists of the Western Sudan.

Sunni Ali captured Timbuktu, the key trading city in the region, in 1468. He killed many of the Muslim scholars who hated his traditional religion, which they saw as paganism. He then captured Jenne after a great campaign that is

said to have lasted seven years, seven months, and seven days. To the south he captured Tetanga and Hombori; to the east he conquered Kebbi. This greatly expanded the territory of Songhay and brought in vast wealth.

Sunni Ali acquired a reputation as a great warrior and an inspiring leader during his reign of twenty-eight years. Someone once described him as "always the conqueror, never the conquered." He was so successful that many believed he used magic to win his battles. Legend states that he made his soldiers and horses take the magic charm *korte* before battles. This made them invisible to the enemy and gave them the power to fly. He himself is said to have been able to change into a vulture. His death from drowning was also viewed as a mysterious, spiritual event.

Sunni Ali laid the foundation for the Songhay Empire. Through his military campaigns, he brought many ethnic groups into the empire, but his accomplishments were not all on the battlefield. His reign brought peace, stability, and prosperity.

Sunni Ali created a system of administration to unify the state and its many different ethnic groups. He divided the empire into provinces, which war leaders ruled as governors. He assigned army generals to maintain law and order in important provinces. In conquered

Since the arrival of Islam in the Western Sudan, beautiful mosques have been centers of worship and learning. This mosque at Jenne was built about one hundred years ago in an ancient style. Seen here are worshippers of many ethnic backgrounds, leaving after Friday service.

provinces that accepted Songhay's authority, he allowed local leaders to stay in power. He dealt harshly with the Muslims of Timbuktu, who despised him, but treated those of Jenne, who accepted his authority, with tolerance and respect.

Sunni Ali did not completely ignore Islam. He accepted the religion and adopted a Muslim name, but he refused to give absolute loyalty to Islam. In fact, Islam influenced only a minority of his people. The majority of the Songhay retained their traditional religion. This is one of the main reasons why most Arab historians have harsh views of Sunni Ali's career. He has been called a tyrant, an oppressor.

19

However, a closer look at his reign shows that he successfully took up a challenge that still faces many of today's African leaders—the challenge of building a nation, of uniting different ethnic and language groups into a single state.

▼ ASKIA MUHAMMAD TOURÉ ▼

Sunni Ali was succeeded by his son, Abu Bakr, who was soon overthrown by one of his father's trusted generals, Askia (General) Muhammad Touré. Askia Muhammad then established a third Songhay dynasty, called Askia, in 1493.

To strengthen his position and gain acceptance for his dynasty, Askia Muhammad did two important things. He killed or exiled the key figures of the two previous dynasties, and he embraced Islam. He treated the Muslims very well and appointed many of them as advisers.

To strengthen his status, Askia Muhammad made a famous pilgrimage, or *hajj*, to Mecca between 1496 and 1498. He was accompanied by 1,000 infantry and 5,000 horsemen carrying 300,500 pieces of gold. He spent much of his wealth for the relief of the poor in the Middle East and North Africa. He also built a hostel for Sudanese pilgrims in Cairo. The pilgrimage brought Askia Muhammad the fame, respect, and acceptance he sought. He was given the titles Al-hajj and Khalifatu Biladi al-Takrur (Caliph of the Blacks). He was also given the

appropriate uniform—a green gown, a green cap, a white turban, and an Arabian sword. He became the acknowledged head of a community of Muslim believers.

Askia Muhammad's acceptance of Islam also began an era of diplomatic relations between the Middle East and Songhay. He attracted famous Islamic scholars to Songhay. Among them was Muhammad al-Maghili, author of *The Obligations of Princes*, a book about the duties and responsibilities of a dedicated Muslim leader.

Askia Muhammad embraced Islam with a major purpose in mind: to convert the Songhay to Islam. Because the economic life of the empire depended on the activities of Muslim traders in the towns, it was important to accept and support them. But most rural Songhay people were not traders and kept their religion. The result was tension between the Songhay and the Muslims. Askia Muhammad wanted to promote stability by encouraging everyone to unite as Muslims.

When he returned from Mecca, Askia Muhammad set an example by faithfully observing the beliefs of Islam. These were the five daily prayers, the fast during the month of Ramadan, the giving of *zakat* (alms), and the practice of veiling women (*purdah*) and having them stay in a section of the house isolated from strangers.

He appointed Qadis, Islamic judges, to run

the courts and apply Sharia, Islamic law. Qadis, assisted by legal experts, were established throughout the empire. They were appointed for life by the king. It was the king's duty as a Muslim to keep Islamic justice, but the vast majority of the Songhay continued to use traditional law. This law was kept by local authorities together with spiritualists and diviners.

Askia Muhammad tried to change, but failed to eliminate completely, the traditional beliefs of the Songhay. His religious reform was most successful in Timbuktu, which was already dominated by Islam. But in Gao and Kukya, centers of the empire, the Songhay retained their beliefs.

Askia Muhammad did greatly improve the intellectual life of Songhay. Arab scholars came from North Africa and the Middle East to settle in Timbuktu and Jenne. Askia Muhammad encouraged Islamic education at all levels. By one account, he built as many as 180 Koranic schools in Timbuktu alone. The Sankore University there developed a reputation for scholarship in rhetoric, logic, Islamic law, grammar, astronomy, history, and geography.

Askia Muhammad also expanded the territory of Songhay. He reformed the military and established a professional, full-time army. He captured Taghaza, a strategic salt-mining town in the Sahara Desert. He conquered Mali after a long war and made the Malinke pay tribute. He

Islamic education was strongly encouraged five hundred years ago, during the Songhay Empire. This tradition continues today with students like Kolado Bocoum, seen here writing Arabic on a washable tablet used for exercises.

then defeated the Fulani to the southwest. Marching eastward to Lake Chad, he captured the Hausa states of Gobir, Kano, Katsina, and Zaria. To the west he conquered Tekrur, and to the north, the Aïr oasis, which had been controlled by the Tuareg. Today Songhay people are still found in the Aïr oasis. By the end of his campaigns, Askia Muhammad had turned Songhay into the largest empire ever known in the Western and Central Sudan.

Such an expanded state required efficient

administration. Askia Muhammad retained the provincial structure created by Sunni Ali, but he grouped the empire into four regions. Each region was ruled by a governor, usually a relative, who assumed the title Koi or Fari. Each region was then divided into provinces ruled by administrators who were directly responsible to the governors. Sunni Ali appointed harbormasters and customs officials for the port cities of Gao and Kebara. He directly ruled by the central government with the assistance of a council of ministers. Each minister was responsible for separate aspects of administration. Vassal states, administered by local chiefs who swore allegiance to the king, included Kano, Katsina, and Agades. Important towns enjoyed a degree of independence, with their own local chiefs and government officials.

Askia Muhammad established one system of weights and measures for the entire empire, made laws against cheating in business transactions, and appointed royal officials to enforce his rules. He established royal estates throughout the empire, worked by slaves and supervised by estate officials. Each estate was responsible for producing a certain amount of a particular crop each year—corn, rice, fish, or sorghum. Artisans were also organized and required to manufacture boots, spears, and arrows for the military. To add to the income from the estates, Askia

During the Songhay Empire, specialist metal and leather workers supplied items to the military. Here the Kassé family of blacksmiths are seen in their workshop in Jenne.

Muhammad collected tribute from vassals and customs duties from traders. He created an efficient economy that not only generated income but also produced the goods needed by the population and the military.

Askia Muhammad's success can be measured by the peace and stability of his reign. The increase in trade and commerce, particularly the trans-Saharan trade, improved the standard of living. Cities such as Timbuktu, Gao, and Jenne grew and enjoyed economic prosperity. Askia Muhammad encouraged agriculture, industry, and trade, which was the backbone of the economy. Songhay exported gold, ivory, and slaves to the west coast and North Africa and imported European goods, horses, and arms from North Africa.

Jenne is situated on an island in the Niger River. Boats such as these have always been essential to trade.

SONGHAY ADMINISTRATORS

The Songhay Executive Council

Katisi-Farma (Minister of Finance)

Asari-Mundya (Minister of Justice)

Hikoy (Minister of the Navy)

Farma (Minister of the Army)

Korey-Farma (Minister of Foreign Affairs)

Sao-Farma (Minister of Forestry)

Hari-Farma (Minister of Rivers, Lakes, and Fisheries)

Kari-Farma (Chief Priest)

Songhay reached its peak in power under Askia Muhammad. He was a fair leader and a devout Muslim. Arab historians have been generous in their view of his career. He has been called "The Great." Askia Muhammad's thirty-five-year reign ended with his death in 1528.

In 1591 Songhay was destroyed by Moroccans led by El Mansur. This event was witnessed by the Songhay author, Mahmoud Kati. His book, the *Tarikh al-Fettash*, provides a personal account of both the greatness and the destruction of Songhay.▲

chapter

2

RELIGION AND SOCIETY

BEFORE THE ARRIVAL OF ISLAM, THE SONGHAY worshiped many gods, goddesses, and objects, but the focus of their religion was their ancestors. Like many other African societies, they believed in communication between the dead and the living. Ancestors, they thought, stood between the living and God and helped them communicate. The Songhay believed that, in order to have peace, stability, good health, and prosperity, it was necessary to stay in harmony with nature and God. They achieved this harmony by communicating with their ancestors and the many spirits and gods. Diviners and spiritualists also helped the Songhay to achieve this harmony by interpreting spiritual forces. They are still used for this purpose today.

As in the past, believers in Songhay tradi-

Family relationships are very important to the Songhay. According to Muslim and Songhay traditions, men may have more than one wife. Having large families provides many workers for family enterprises. Seen here is the expert Songhay tailor Dani Traoré with his wife, children, and some of their friends.

tional religion today worship Harakoy Dikko, goddess of the Niger River; Dongo, god of thunder; Maalu, deity of lightning; Moussa Nyori, the divine hunter who controls the formation of the clouds; Hausakoy, god of iron; Mahamane Surgu, god of war; Faran Baru Koda, the spirit child who controls the fate of millet fields; Nya Beri, the Great Mother who created the spirits of cold and death; and Ndebbi, God's messenger who brings information to diviners.

The Songhay also have great strength, vitality, and hope because of their strong tradition of kinship. A Songhay is never alone. He or she is

POSSESSION

Getting in touch with spirits and ancestors is done through possession. This ancient ceremony uses music and vision to establish the link that the Songhay believe exists between the human and spiritual worlds.

Many Songhay believe that the world consists of seven heavens, seven hells, and the earth. The earth has two parts, the social one of the living and the eternal one of the spirits. God lives in the most distant heaven. Next to God, in the sixth heaven, lives his messenger, Ndebbi. Ancestors or angels occupy heavens two to five. The spirits occupy the first heaven, the one nearest earth. Since spirits and human beings

These musicians are playing at a possession ceremony in Niger. Also seen are a spirit medium (above) and a Songhay man dancing during possession (right).

are so close to each other, they interact constantly. In the possession ceremony, this closeness is emphasized and strengthened, and the spirits are prepared to resolve human problems.

During the ceremony, the spirit enters the body of a medium, which means that it takes possession of a living person's body. As the spirit enters the body, the medium shakes uncontrollably until the spirit has completely taken over the body. The spirit then dances, screams, and speaks in a language that is understood only by the chief priest of possession, the Zima.

The ceremony is organized by a special troupe, led by the Zima. The troupe gathers the animals that are to be sacrificed and hires musicians and praise-singers. The Zima directs the ceremony and interprets the strange sounds made by the spirit.

The spirit selects a medium by making a person ill. When someone becomes ill in Songhay society and all attempts to cure the illness fail, it is assumed that the person has been chosen as a medium. The person must undergo possession to be cured. Thereafter, he or she is obliged to pay homage to the spirits for life.

Possession is performed for many reasons: to deal with personal problems such as infertility; to help one choose a spouse or a career; or to relieve social problems such as drought, famine, disease, or floods.

surrounded by a network of relatives, neighbors, and peers of the same age group who share duties and responsibilities. All these people contribute to the well-being of the individual and the group.

The family was (and to some extent still is) the basis of all Songhay social life and daily activities. The Songhay place strong emphasis on clans or lineages, groups of families whose heads are descended from the same ancestor. This focus on clans demonstrates the attachment of the Songhay to the values of kinship. Most of the early Songhay clans, with the exception of the Maiga, were of Soninke origin. They include the Ture, Sylla, Tunkara, Cisse, and Drame. This mixture of Soninke, Berber, Malinke, Gobir, and Hausa ancestry make it difficult to tell the true character of early Songhay society.

Early Songhay society was very hierarchical. It consisted of the nobility (members of the ruling class, the Sunnis, the Askias, and the merchants), freemen, artisans, peasants, and slaves. Nearly all the societies of the West and Central Sudan at this time developed similar class structures. But the Songhay were unique because they were the only society to have a nobility that focused on warfare and administration. The Songhay nobility lived in the towns, while most of the population, the peasants, slaves, and

Today, as in the past, there are many differences between the lifestyles of urban and rural Songhay. This rural Songhay homestead is in Sohanci, Niger.

artisans, lived in the countryside. Slaves, acquired mostly from wars, performed domestic labor. Under Askia Muhammad, they were involved in producing goods on the royal estates. Peasant communities settled around the royal estates. Their round, earthen houses with thatched roofs were spread throughout the countryside.

▼ THE KING ▼

Early in their history, the Songhay were ruled by kings. The king was considered the father of his people and the source of wealth and of the fertility of the land, herds, and community. The king was also the commander-in-chief who led his people in battle. He was regarded as semidivine. His subjects were required to bow in his presence. Such respect and reverence is still associated with royalty in some African societies.

33

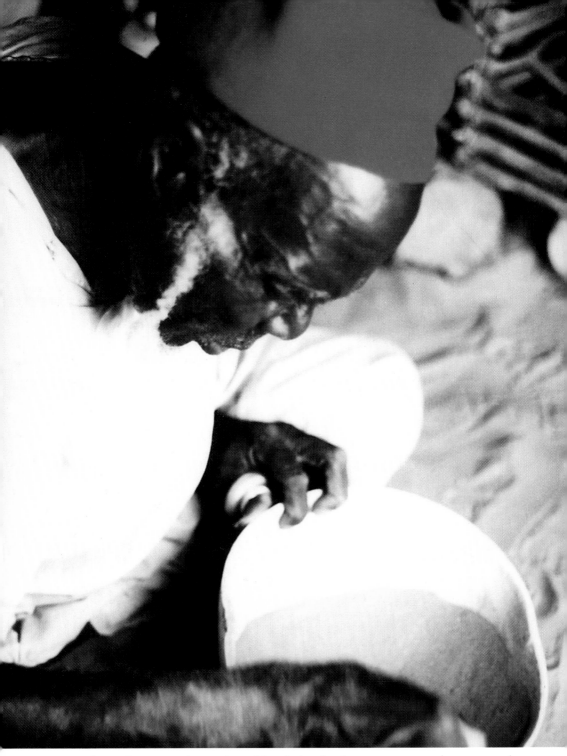

Songhay religious traditions have blended with Islam. Here a Songhay spiritualist prepares traditional medicines while wearing the red fez favored by Muslims.

Under the Sunnis, the monarchy relied heavily on magic, sorcery, and divination to perform its duties. With the introduction of Islam, Songhay royalty gradually began to decrease the traditional religious importance of the king. Under the Askis, royalty became much more Islamic. Islam and Songhay beliefs seem to have coexisted peacefully, with neither completely replacing the other. Each religion dominated at different times, depending on the character of the king.

The Songhay king lived in Gao. He was assisted by a large court, the Sunna, which included family members, state officials, and the *griots*. The *griots* functioned as the king's heralds and official recordkeepers. They also recorded history, especially in the form of songs, epic poems, and stories. These were both entertaining and educational.

The king's palace was surrounded by a wall and had a central courtyard. The king's wives and children lived in separate sections, attended by slaves. Usually the throne passed to the king's eldest son, but sometimes it passed to the king's brother. The new king was given his staff of office by the Sunna and enthroned in the ancient capital, Kukya.

▼ THE MILITARY ▼

Askia Muhammad's professional army was

led by the Songhay nobility. They formed the cavalry, which was the elite corps. Since horses were expensive and difficult to get, only the nobility had access to them. Armed with lances, sabers, and arrows, Songhay horsemen wore iron breastplates beneath their battle tunics.

The infantry, the largest section of the military, was made up of slaves, peasants, and the lesser nobility. They were armed with spears, bows and arrows, and leather or copper shields. The size of the Songhay army, at the time of the famous battle of Tondibi in 1591, was estimated at 30,000 infantry men and 10,000 horsemen. It was the largest force in the Western Sudan.

▼ EDUCATION ▼

Songhay transformed the intellectual culture of the region. Before the arrival of Islam, the Songhay had no formal education. Education was part of one's upbringing and the responsibility of the family. The Songhay elders were regarded as the safekeepers and teachers of knowledge and wisdom. Children were encouraged to remain close to and respect their elders so that they could learn ideas and values that would help them become good citizens.

Askia Muhammad passionately fought against illiteracy in the Sudan. His pilgrimage to Mecca and his devotion to Islam attracted Arab scholars from North Africa and the Middle East to

Songhay. Timbuktu became an educational and commercial center.

Elementary or primary students were taught to read and recite the Koran, the sacred Islamic text. Advanced students concentrated on such subjects as theology (Tawhid), interpretation (Tafsir), traditions of the prophet (Hadith), and Islamic law (Fikh). They also learned grammar, rhetoric, logic, astrology, history, and geography. Sankore University was renowned as the leading research and learning center in the region.

Sankore University produced many important scholars. We depend on their work for much of our knowledge of the early history of the West and Central Sudan. Among the most notable were Muhammad Kati (b.1468), author of *Tarikh al-Fattash* (Chronicle of the Seeker of Knowledge); Abdelrahman As-Sadi (b.1569), who wrote *Tarikh as-Sudan* (Chronicle of the Western Sudan); and Ahmad Baba (b.1556), who wrote a biographical dictionary and as many as fifty books on Islamic law.

Askia Muhammad gave scholarships to Songhay students to study in Morocco and Egypt. They returned to contribute to an intellectual movement that spread throughout the entire Sudan in the 1400s and 1500s. What became known as the Timbuktu tradition of learning spread to and dominated the cities of the Sudan into the 1800s.▲

chapter

3

THE ECONOMY

THE SONGHAY ECONOMY HAD TWO SEPARATE,
but equally important, sectors—rural agriculture
and urban trading. In addition to the royal
estates, large estates were owned by the princes,
urban Ulama (Muslim religious leaders), and
merchants. They were worked by slaves and
peasants, who were organized into farming
villages. Agriculture was so profitable that some
people left their profession during the growing
season to farm. Anyone, including the peasants,
could farm for profit by renting land at reason-
able rents from the landowners.

The cities of Timbuktu, Gao, and Jenne
made large profits from the trans-Saharan trade.
This trade activity caused urban areas to expand
and grow. By the 1400s these cities had become
major commercial centers, inhabited mostly by
foreign merchants.

Jenne remains a busy and important trade center today. Caravans still travel across the desert (above), but many traders and vendors at the Monday Market in Jenne now arrive by car or truck (below).

This Songhay tailor has set up business in Tillaberi, Niger. His sign says,
"HERE IS YOUR TAILOR—MEN AND WOMEN."

Timbuktu, conquered by Sunni Ali in 1468, reached the peak of its power in the 1500s, with a population of about 200,000. Besides the merchants, the city had many artisans—weavers, tailors, tanners, shoemakers, goldsmiths, potters, salt makers, and manufacturers of weapons and farming tools. Leo Africanus, a traveler who spent some time in Timbuktu, described what he saw: "Here are many shops of [craftsmen] and merchants [who have woven] linen and cotton cloth. To them the North African merchants bring the cloth of Europe. The inhabitants and especially the strangers residing there are exceedingly rich." He also said, "More profit is made from the book trade than from any other line of business."

Gao, on the bend of the Niger River, started to grow in importance early in the eighth century. The surrounding fertile land sustained agriculture, and the river made fishing possible. Three important trade routes from Morocco, Algeria, and Egypt came together in the city of Gao. The Muslim traveler Ibn Batuta visited in 1353 and recorded this impression: "Gao is a large city—one of the finest towns in the Sudan. It is also one of the biggest and best provisioned towns, with rice in plenty, milk, and fish." Leo Africanus described the city as also "full of exceedingly rich merchants."

The third major urban center, Jenne, is an

During the time of the great empires of the Western Sudan, its cities were amongst the world's most important centers of knowledge. In Timbuktu, the book trade was once the most profitable business. Seen here are some beautiful pages from an African Koran.

island in the Niger. It too benefited from agriculture and trade. Because it was close to the forest region to the south, it served as the first exchange point for traders from the south.

These three cities—Timbuktu, Gao, and Jenne—accounted for much of economic, educational, and cultural wealth of Songhay. This prosperity was made possible by the flourishing agriculture and trade, the two basic sectors of the Songhay economy.▲

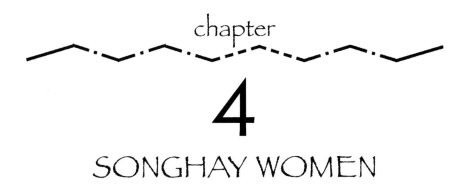

chapter

4

SONGHAY WOMEN

THE HISTORY OF MEDIEVAL SONGHAY DOES not say much about the status and role of women. This is not surprising, since Songhay, like so many other African societies, is strongly patriarchal, or male-dominated. Developments and events were seen and created from the point of view of men. History was recorded by male scholars.

Many Muslim societies veiled their women. Under the system of privacy, called *purdah*, women were not to be seen in public, or by men other than their husbands. They were restricted to the house and had to wear a veil whenever they left home.

In most Islamic societies, men control political, economic, and social power. The practice of polygyny, in which a man may have more than one wife, is allowed by both Islam

Today, Songhay women are active in every aspect of society. This elder, with the tattooed lips and gums once common among the Songhay nobility, is seated with her grandson Haber in a doorway of the Gano family home.

and the traditional Songhay religion. This practice places women in an inferior position in the family. In some strict Islamic societies, women are thought to be of low intelligence. This belief is expressed in the following saying, "The minds of women never develop fully; they are never ready for serious study."

The cultural domination of women has other effects. Among the Songhay, a person's loyalty is to the male lineage, a group of descendents of the same male ancestor. Men and women are often more attached to their brother than to their spouse. Under this custom, men and women do not share their possessions. In divorce, which is very common among the

Songhay, the woman loses her children to her husband's lineage.

In the past, women were confined to domestic tasks. In modern Songhay society women are found in almost every occupation, such as agriculture, trade, and industry.

Songhay women do enjoy a significant degree of power and independence in one area: that of the spiritual world. Knowledge of divination and the use of traditional medicines gives Songhay women high status. In the hierarchy of deities, the most important is Nya Beri, "Great Mother." She is goddess of the spirit of the cold. She is responsible for miscarriages, stillbirths, and death. Nya Beri is the most dangerous of Songhay spirits. She is bigger and stronger than any Songhay man, and she is invincible. For instance, Nya Beri can stare directly at the sun and still see. She is able to predict the future by staring into fresh milk. She sees into the past by looking at blood. Nya Beri sees all and knows all. Another female goddess is Harakoy Dikko, the goddess of the Niger, the source of life-giving water.▲

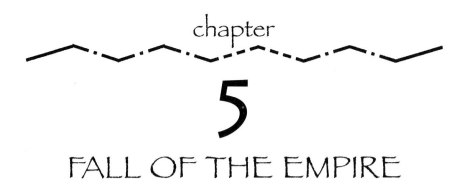

chapter

5

FALL OF THE EMPIRE

BY THE END OF THE 1400s, SONGHAY HAD many features of modern civilization. It had good government, a strong economy, a judicial system, education and communication systems, religion, and urbanization. The peace and stability of the reign of Askia Muhammad allowed the Songhay and their neighbors to prosper in many ways. Had this trend continued, many argue, Songhay might have survived to become a modern African state that guaranteed all the essential human freedoms. Unfortunately, history did not work out that way.

At the age of eighty-five, Askia Muhammad was removed from the throne by his eldest son, Musa, and exiled to a remote island in the Niger River. From 1528 to 1549, four rulers occupied the throne of Songhay: Askia Musa (1528–33), Askia Bankuri (1533–37), Askia

Ismail (1537–39), and Askia Ishak I (1539–49). In this time, several vassal states declared their independence.

Songhay prestige and hope were restored briefly during the reign of Askia Dawd (1549–82). Though the empire was near the point of total collapse, Dawd succeeded in strengthening Songhay. He regained most of the territories, and suppressed a rebellion by the Tuareg. The three Askias who succeeded him, Muhammad III (1582–86), Askia Muhammad Bani (1586–88), and Askia Ishak II (1588–91), were weak, inefficient, and immoral. Under these weak rulers, the unity of the empire began to disintegrate.

Songhay had for centuries attracted the attention and envy of North African countries, particularly Morocco. On a few occasions, the sultan of Morocco attempted to seize the rich salt-mining town of Taghaza. In 1584, Sultan Mulay Ahmed (Al-Mansur, "the victorious") attempted to invade Songhay, but failed. However, at the battle of Tondibi in April 1591, the Moroccan forces defeated the Songhay and captured Timbuktu and Gao. The Songhay ruling class fled and resettled west of the Niger bend, far from the influence of the conquering Moroccans.

Songhay became a province of Morocco. The sultan appointed governors called Pashas, who

quickly established a reputation for corruption and immorality. They plundered the wealth and resources of Songhay. Gold and livestock were taken to Morocco. Little attention was paid to the political, economic, and cultural well-being of Songhay.

The trans-Saharan trade declined and the region could not recover from the devastations of the Moroccan invasion. The economic and intellectual glories of Timbuktu, Gao, and Jenne disappeared. Many of Sankore University's students died or fled, and thousands of manuscripts were destroyed. In the words of the Sudanese historian As-Sadi, ". . . security gave place to danger, wealth to poverty, distress and calamities, and violence succeeded tranquility. Everywhere men destroyed each other, in every place and in every direction there was plundering . . . , disorder was spread everywhere, rising to the highest degree of intensity."

▼ POSTCLASSICAL SONGHAY ▼

Songhay was the last major empire of the Western Sudan. For the next two centuries, large empires were replaced by numerous small states—Segu, Tuareg, Hausa, Borno, Bamana, and Mossi.

The Songhay people split into small units: Kokoro, Karma, Ayoro, Gorouol, Namaro, Tera, Sorko, and Dargal. They migrated in different

directions, where they met, defeated, and partially absorbed indigenous populations into their own culture. In some areas they themselves were absorbed by other peoples. For example, a group of Sorko fishermen entered the Sokoto River valley of Nigeria, where they intermarried with the local people and eventually became part of the local culture, losing their Songhay identity. Most Songhay, however, remained in the region of the Niger River bend. There they were eventually absorbed into new religious and political groups.

The Songhay ruling class that had fled westward and resettled soon established a small state. They led wealthy lifestyles and revived the class divisions that had characterized classical Songhay society. A new class of nobility also emerged, the warrior nobles. They looked down upon and refused to participate in any manual labor. The warrior nobles were also different because they owned slaves, cattle, and other forms of material wealth. The gaps between the nobility, the common people, and the slaves widened.

The Tuareg, vassals of Askia Muhammad, asserted themselves and defeated various Songhay groups. The original home of the Tuareg was in northeast Africa. From there they began a series of migrations in the seventh century, spreading across the Sahara Desert. They

This part of Africa has always been home to many different peoples. Successful states in the region made peace and traded with others of different background. Seen here are Tuareg nomads (above), and two Fulani women who are visiting a Songhay village to sell milk (below).

specialized in camel herding and soon became masters of the desert, running camel caravans that carried goods such as salt and copper. By the 1100s Timbuktu was a major Tuareg destination and trading base. The emergence of the Tuareg as a political power in the Western and Central Sudan began at about the same time as the Moroccan conquest. By the middle of the 1600s, they had settled in the eastern part of the Niger Valley, in the area between Gao and Dendi. For much of the 1700s, the Tuareg engaged in bitter conflicts with the Arma, descendants of the Moroccan Pashas. At the end of the century they captured Timbuktu.

From about 1750, Fulani nomads invaded the region and established a strong foothold in Diagoru. From Diagoru they made frequent raids upon the many groups of Songhay, particularly the Dargol and Tera. At the beginning of the 1800s the Fulani started a *jihad* aimed at forcing the locals to convert to Islam. This resulted in the creation of several strong Islamic states in the Sudan, including the Caliphate of Hamdallahi (sometimes referred to as the state of Maccina). Founded by Seku Ahmadu in 1819, this state covered the entire region between Jenne and Timbuktu. It was soon eclipsed by another Islamic state founded by Al-Hajj Umar, the Tukulor Empire. It extended east of the Niger and into much of the lands between the Niger and Senegal Rivers.

The Malinke, descendants of the old Mali Empire, led from 1879 by Samouri Touré, extended their state from Sierra Leone in the west to Côte d'Ivoire in the east, covering about half of the Western Sudan. The Songhay were absorbed into these new states, becoming vassals of the Fulani. By the late 1800s, therefore, virtually the whole of Songhay territory was under the Tuareg and the Fulani.

▼ COLONIAL RULE ▼

The rule of the Fulani and Tuareg was, however, short-lived. By the 1850s the Europeans penetrated into the interior of this region and threatened the indigenous states. The Europeans had a strong presence on the West African coast long before the collapse of classical Songhay. In the mid-1800s they became increasingly interested in the interior and began to interfere in the daily affairs of African states. They also increased in number. The Portuguese came first; then came the Spanish, followed by the British, French, Dutch, Germans, and Belgians.

Driven by a combination of economic, political, and religious factors, the Europeans were determined to gain greater control of Africa. The French and the British focused

much of their attention on the region that included Songhay territory. By the 1880s, what became known as the European Scramble for Africa had started. The French focused on the Niger bend, home of the Songhay. There they had to contend with the new political powers in the region, the Malinke under Samouri Touré and the Tukulor Empire led by Al-Hajj Umar.

The superiority of French weapons resulted in the colonists' defeat of the Sudan. By the beginning of the twentieth century, France controlled all the territory from Senegal in the west to Burkina Faso in the east. This area included the Songhay.

The Tuareg mounted a strong resistance to French presence until 1899. The Songhay, along with the Zerma, who were culturally similar to the Songhay, were among the first to mount a resistance against the French. In 1905–06 the Songhay launched a series of revolts, but they were defeated.

The Songhay found themselves concentrated in the French colonial territories of Mali, Niger, and Upper Volta (later named Burkina Faso). Songhay chiefs were absorbed into the new French system of local government, several of them becoming chiefs of cantons—the lowest of the administrative units in the political system. Perhaps because of the fierce resistance of the Zerma-Songhay, the French were forced to

reckon with them. This gave them greater op-
portunities in the administration.

The French deliberately discouraged the
emergence of an educated class of Africans. Up
to the 1950s, the majority of those who had
access to education were Zerma. The Songhay,
along with other African groups, were often
arrested and imprisoned. They were denied
political rights, forced to work without pay, and
imprisoned at the will of French officials.

Traditional farmers such as the Gobibi
suddenly were forced to grow only cash crops
like peanuts. These were sold abroad to profit
the French government. The French imposed
excessive taxes on Africans. This forced them to
labor on public projects such as the construction
of roads, bridges, and railroads to earn the cash
to pay the taxes. To escape this oppression, the
Songhay migrated to neighboring countries. The
vast majority went to the British colony of the
Gold Coast (later named Ghana), where they
worked as laborers.

The French failed in their attempts to en-
courage young Songhay to work for the benefit
of their government and discourage migration.
Few Songhay were willing to work for a state
that refused to pay them fairly for their labor.

French colonial rule, like that of the British,
ended in most parts of West Africa in the 1960s.
Niger became fully independent in 1960. Before

Today, Songhay people live in many parts of the world. Seen here are two Songhay traders on 125th Street, in New York City.

gaining full independence, it had successively been made an "autonomous territory," an Overseas Territory of France, and then a self-governing republic.

Although French colonization was often brutal and unfair, many Songhay claim that it had little impact on their culture. So long and proud is Songhay history that the bad times under the French seem like just a brief moment in their past. In their words, "The white man comes and goes like the morning mist on the Niger River."▲

Songhay nobles can be recognized by their dignified dress and behavior. They are highly respected. This elder from Tillaberi, Niger stands in front of a sacred canopy.

chapter

6

A VIEW OF THE FUTURE

MODERN SONGHAY IS A SOCIALLY EXCLUSIVE society. Classes are still a fundamental feature, as in the classical period. The nobility conduct themselves with dignity and a sense of exclusivity. They dress differently, usually in white robes, and carry a wooden cane. They are very reserved and rarely speak, except through a third party. All these attributes contribute to the awe and respect that the nobility receive in Songhay society. The nobility also control political power. For example, only a member of the nobility is qualified to be a chief. The chief is seen as combining two unique qualities—the wisdom to govern, and the *fula* (hat) of inner strength and determination. A chief undergoes a transformation in status, becoming the earthly form of the divine.

The Songhay identify wisdom with age.

According to them, "The mind of a child is not developed; he is therefore not ready for serious study. The mind of an adolescent is not developed; he is therefore not ready for serious study. . . . A man's mind can begin to receive important knowledge when he is forty years of age, but it is not until a man reaches the age of sixty that he is fully ready to learn."

The modern Songhay society is based on the ideas of two different cultures. Islam and traditional forces still coexist.

The Songhay use Islam to unify and strengthen their government and to tighten the bond between the king and his subjects. The Songhay king is considered the last in a line of rulers that began when Allah gave the Prophet Muhammad the *fula*, or hat, which is the symbol of leadership in the Islamic world. Although powerful and worshipped by his people, the king is, in turn, accountable to God.

On the other hand, there is an attempt among traditional Songhay believers to strengthen traditional practices by deeply rooting them in history. The most powerful diviners of modern Songhay live in Wanzerbe, in southwest Niger Republic. They consider themselves the descendants of Sunni Ali Ber, who is said to have passed his knowledge down through his descendants until it reached the *sohancis* (diviners) of Wanzerbe. There are many *sohancis* in

Sohancis maintain special spirit houses, where they practice their profession. This spirit house is in Tillaber, Niger.

Wanzerbe, each maintaining a private spirit house. The most powerful *sohanci*, considered the product of a union of a *sohanci* and a witch, is the *guunu*. The expert in circumcision rites, the *guunu* of Wanzerbe is a very busy person. He performs circumcision not only for the Songhay, but also for their neighbors, the Hausa, Bamana, Fulani, and Mossi.

Circumcision is required by Islam, yet it is also performed by diviners who represent pre-Islamic belief. While this area of Niger is famous for its *sohancis*, it is also the site of the Friday Mosque, the most sacred building among the Songhay of the region. The Friday Mosque is both a religious and social place. These examples show how pre-Islamic and Islamic beliefs are blended in Songhay today.

It is clear that modern Songhay has retained

The Friday Mosque, a detail of which is seen here, is the most sacred building of the Songhay of Niger.

many of the traditions and cultures of its ancient past. Colonialism was indeed "like the morning mist on the Niger." Now part of a larger political body, the Songhay have not lost their sense of history. Though largely confined to the rural parts of the Republics of Mali and Niger, they are a proud people with a rich culture. They are inspired by the knowledge that in centuries past their ancestors created one of the world's great civilizations.▲

Glossary

diviner Priest and seer.

dynasty Succession of rulers of the same family.

fula Hat (symbol) of office.

guunu Chief sorcerer, expert in circumcision.

hierarchical Graded through rank.

Hikoy Commander of the navy.

jihad Holy war to convert others to Islam.

kolanut Nut containing caffeine.

korte Magic charm.

pagan Believer in more than one god.

Qadi Islamic judge, appointed for life.

Ramadan An annual Islamic fasting period.

rhetoric The art of speaking or writing.

Sharia Islamic system of law.

sohanci Diviner.

Sunni Songhay title meaning "liberator."

theology Study of religion.

tribute Payment made to acknowledge submission to another ruler.

Ulama Muslim religious leader.

vassal Person or state under the authority of a medieval lord.

For Further Reading

Boahen, Adu. *Topics in West African History.*
London: Longman, 1986.

Buah, F.K. *West Africa Since A.D. 1000.* Volume
1. London: Macmillan, 1977.

Chou, Daniel, and Skinner, Elliott. *A Glorious
Age in Africa: The Story of Three Great African
Empires.* Trenton, N.J.: African World Press,
Inc., 1990.

Harris, Joseph E. *Africans and Their History.* New
York: New American Library, 1972.

McKissick, Patricia, and McKissick, Frederick.
*The Royal Kingdoms of Ghana, Mali and
Songhay: Life in Medieval Africa.* New York:
Henry Holt & Co., 1994.

Osae, T.A., and Nwabara, S.N. *A Short History
of West Africa, A.D. 1000–1800.* Volume 1.
London: Hodder & Stoughton, 1980.

Shinnie, Margaret. *Ancient African Kingdoms.*
New York: New American Library, 1965.

Stride, G.T., and Ifeka, C. *Peoples and Empires of
West Africa.* London: Thomas Nelson & Sons,
1977.

Index

64   SONGHAY

ABOUT THE AUTHOR
Tunde Adeleke, a Nigerian, is Director of Africana Studies at Loyola University, New Orleans. He holds degrees in African and African-American history and his research focuses on African history and culture and African-American topics. He has published extensively in journals, including *The Journal of Negro Education*, *Biography*, and *The Journal of Thought*. He is currently completing a biography of the African-American leader Martin R. Delany and a critique of late nineteenth-century African-American nationalism.

PHOTO CREDITS
Cover, pp. 30, 31, 33, 34, 40, 55, 56, 59, 60 © Paul Stoller; pp. 8, 12, 15, 19, 23, 25, 26, 29, 39 bottom, 44, 50 bottom © Adria La Violette; p. 39 top © Royal Geographical Society/Mike Foster; p. 42 © Werner Forman Archive/Art Resource, London/New York; p. 50 top © ANAKO Editions/Jean Pierre Valentin.

CONSULTING EDITOR
Gary N. van Wyk, Ph.D.

LAYOUT AND DESIGN
Kim Sonsky